Religious Views Of The Society Of Friends

Howard M. Jenkins

Alpha Editions

This Edition Published in 2021

ISBN: 9789354448591

Design and Setting By
Alpha Editions
www.alphaedis.com
Email – info@alphaedis.com

As per information held with us this book is in Public Domain.
This book is a reproduction of an important historical work. Alpha Editions
uses the best technology to reproduce historical work in the same manner
it was first published to preserve its original nature. Any marks or number
seen are left intentionally to preserve its true form.

RELIGIOUS VIEWS

OF

THE SOCIETY OF FRIENDS

BY HOWARD M. JENKINS.

A Paper Read at the World's Congress of Religions
at Chicago, Ninth month 19, 1893.

(THIRD EDITION)

PHILADELPHIA, PA.
Friends' General Conference Advancement Committee
1913

RELIGIOUS VIEWS OF THE SOCIETY OF FRIENDS.

The Religious Society of Friends, represented in part by this gathering in the Congress of Religions, arose in England in the middle of the Seventeenth Century. Its first and most eminent minister, George Fox, the son of a weaver, himself a shoemaker and shepherd, was born in 1624, and began his religious labors somewhat earlier than 1650. Dying in 1690, his forty years of activity had served to awaken, to gather, and to organize the Religious Society for which we speak, and which has now had an existence and a history for nearly two centuries and a half.

The Friends, or Quakers, are an outgrowth from the Protestant movement, and are identified almost entirely with the English-speaking nations. Not now united in one body, those who claim the name, and who regard themselves, notwithstanding variations in views and usage, as having the right to employ it, are found in Great Britain, the Unted States, Canada and Australia, with a few scattered companies elsewhere, mainly the result of missionary effort. Altogether their actual membership is less than 150,000, and in the body which this gathering particularly represents, and which is organized in seven yearly meetings, all in America, there is a membership somewhat less than 25,000. Whether considered, then, as a whole, or in their several divisions, the Friends are in numbers so few as to be almost insignificant when compared with the greater churches of Christendom.

Nevertheless Truth must be weighed, not measured. It does not depend on numbers. The growth which Quakerism has made has been from the humblest beginnings, and has been in spite of, not by the favor of, potentates and hierarchies. No Constantine has swayed great councils in its behalf, and no Charlemagne baptized nations into its communion. Truth, if it be Truth, is greater than Constantine or Charlemagne.

What, then, was the Truth which in 1650 George Fox was declaring? It was that which Jesus signified in his declaration to the woman of Samaria, by the brink of Jacob's well: "God is spirit, and they that worship him must worship him in spirit and in truth." The young preacher called his hearers to a spiritual knowledge of God, and to a real life of religion. He denounced, therefore, the outward, and summoned to the inward. He testified against form, in order that substance might be possessed and enjoyed. William Penn says of the early Friends: "They were directed to the light of Jesus Christ within them, as the seed and leaven of the Kingdom of God; near all, because in all, and God's talent to all. A faithful and true witness and just monitor in every bosom. The gift and grace of God to life and salvation, that appears to all, though few regard it."

Such a conception of Truth is simple, but it is far-reaching. Thrown into the crucible with this powerful solvent, much that was thought and still is thought essential in the systems of religion is consumed. For if religion is simple, and not complex; if it is a practical work, and not a formula of doctrine, or program of ritual; if we may neglect pope and presbyter, and turn away from cloister and cathedral, to hear the voice of God within our own souls, a great structure, dogmatic, ecclesiastical, ceremonial, reared by the hand of man, partly in pride, yet much more in pious sincerity, must decay and disappear.

"Too late I loved thee, O Beauty of ancient days, yet ever new!" says Augustine himself. "And lo! thou wert within, and I abroad searching for thee! Thou wert with me, but I was not with thee."

George Fox did not proclaim a new scheme of salvation, or propose a more elaborate or more attractive system of religion. He conceived that his mission was altogether different. He proposed to return to first principles. He wished to call mankind home. He saw them distracted by confusing voices, such as the Master himself had warned against, the "Lo, here is Christ!" and "Lo, there he is!" and he cited them, therefore to the knowing of Christ within. "For, lo!" declared Jesus, "the Kingdom of God is within you!"

This, then, is that which Quakerism regards as supremely The Truth,—the conception of the Inner Light. It is that which has been called by many names, as the thought, exquisitely simple and beautiful, has unfolded to many minds. It is the Divine Immanence, the Divine Inshining, Immediate Revelation, or, in the words of Penn, "The Light of Christ within, God's gift for man's salvation."

Such a gift, conferred by a just God, must be universal. It must be of every age and all lands. It can be no private property or exclusive possession. So the Quaker believes. To him the touch of man with man, and of nation with nation, results from God's creative act, and God's universal saving light. Such light shone upon the patriarchs, it dwelt with Moses, it enlightened the prophets, it appears in the psalms. Nor yet in Palestine was it confined. The world's life, growing toward the consciousness of its presence, responds to its power in every land, —feebly and slowly, it may be, but yet evidently.

"O Beauty, old yet ever new!
Eternal Voice and Inward Word
The Logos of the Greek and Jew,
The old sphere-music which the Samian heard!

"Nor bounds, nor clime, nor creed thou know'st,
Wide as our need thy favors fall;
The white wings of the Holy Ghost
Stoop, seen or unseen, o'er the heads of all."

Self-evident, self-proved, the Light Within demands no confirmation by bell, book, or candle. Convicting and convincing, it shines alike for prince or pauper, for savant or savage, in palace or desert, on land or on sea.

It must not be thought that the Quaker doctrine of the Inner Light is a doctrine merely,—an intellectual conception, to be theoretically held. Bancroft, when he says in his noble chapter, "the Quaker has but one word, THE INNER LIGHT, the voice of God in the soul," speaks truly, and yet not fully. We must follow his next words, when he says: "That light is reality, and, therefore, in its freedom the highest revelation of truth; it is kindred with the Spirit of God, and therefore, in its purity should be listened to as the guide to virtue; it shines in every man's breast, and, therefore, joins the whole human race in the unity of equal right." "The bent and stress of their ministry," William Penn says further, of the early Friends, "was conversion to God, regeneration, and holiness; not schemes of doctrines and verbal creeds, or new forms of worship, but a leaving off in religion the superfluous, and reducing the ceremonious and formal part, and pressing earnestly the substantial, the necessary, and profitable part to the soul. .. .. They directed people to a principle by which all that they asserted, preached and exhorted others to, might be wrought in them, and known, through experience, to be true." This is the fullness of the great principle of Quakerism, that it is not dogmatic but practical, not barren but fruitful, not held intellectually, but experienced livingly and exemplified in life. "Whosoever heareth these sayings of mine, and doeth them, I will liken him unto a wise man which built his house on a rock." These are the words of the Master. "He hath shown thee, O man, what is good; and what doth the Lord require of thee but to do justly, love mercy, and to walk humbly with thy God?" These are the words of the Prophet. "For as the body without the spirit is dead, so faith without works is dead also." And these are the words of the Apostle.

True Quakerism, then, means both knowledge of God spiritually, and the practical manifestation of that knowledge in this present life. In so far as the Friends fail short in either of these particulars, so far they fail to reach their own ideal. Little or much, so they must be judged.

* * *

The conflict of early Quakerism with the existing systems of England, social and religious, was necessarily acute. The principle of the Friends, and its logical consequences, were at once too simple and too destructive for general acceptance. To admit such a principle would have demanded many humblings of pride, many surrenders of exclusive claims, many renunciations of power. Fox and his followers were opposed and condemned, therefore, and so long as they zealously asserted their faith, were repressed and persecuted. Whether under Oliver or Charles, under Parliament or King, whether the prevailing spirit was rigid or free, sober or dissolute, the Friends proposed too much, and suffered accordingly. Their reward for being two centuries in advance of their time was to be whipped, imprisoned, branded and starved, and—on the gallows of Boston Common—hanged. Not until their own zeal abated, and tolerance of religious differences made some progress, did the Friends obtain quietude, and pass from the condemnation of fanaticism and heresy into the category of a well meaning but peculiar people.

In this storm of persecution from 1650 to 1690, one might think that the other non-conformists of England might have sympathized with the Friends. But they did not. Quakerism has been called "the consummate flower of Puritanism," but no opposition was more harsh than that which the Puritans generally made. Though they were languishing in their horrible gaols for a common cause, the Baptist tinker imprisoned at Bedford had nothing but condemnation for the Quaker shoemaker confined at Lancaster;—the pious and courageous Bunyan, viewing the field at a different, and certainly a narrower angle, was one of Fox's most extreme opponents. They saw the Truth alike at many points, but the spirit of Bunyan's immortal Pilgrim varies from that by which Fox's own life was illustrating the Christian progress. The difference between the two was the difference between their beliefs. Bunyan saw the cross outwardly, Fox embraced it inwardly. The one wanted to be saved from hell, the other to be preserved from sin. *

Was Quakerism, then, and is it now, when faithful to its ideals, at war with the generally accepted systems of religion? Does it secure repose and repute only when it ceases to assert its real mission? Does this handful of plain people presume to take the field against all the hosts of the churches? The answer to these questions

---

*Compare Frederick Storrs Turner, "The Quakers," p. 23.

is both No and Yes. The Friends were called to a particular work. So long as they are entitled to their name they must pursue the course which Fox laid out, and continue to summon the world home. The substance of truth does not change. The duty of calling mankind back to it remains. As the muezzin never tires and never fails, but repeats unvaringly from age to age his summons to prayer, so forever, while it lives, Quakerism is bound to cry to the churches, "Turn within!" "Turn within!" Is this war? It is peace. It is the appeal to the common tie and common ground of all religions. Such a demand goes out in Christian love to lay gentle hold upon every system, every fold, every communion. If, as in the days of Fox, acceptance of the call requires a sacrifice, a surrender of the ceremonial and outward, who shall be blamed for this? Christian, when he reached the place of the cross, found the burden which he had been bearing roll from his shoulders. Will the world, then, coming to the cross, embrace the Truth, and cast off hindering things, or rail, as of old, at the prophets?

* * *

It must be said that the appeal made by the Friends has never been without hopeful response. From the beginning they found fresh courage as they learned that the principle of Truth which appeared to them had appeared to many before. Its germs they found in the philosophy of Plato, and in the writings of the Christian fathers they rejoiced to see it set forth. Tertullian, Justin Martyr, Clement of Alexandria, were among those who had testified to the efficacy and the beauty of the divine indwelling,—Clement, indeed, with an oriental richness of expression, compared with which our own seems poor and meagre. After their day the Church lapsed; in the words of Pressense, such teaching as Clement's was too pure and too spiritual for that age; yet the stream, lost then among the arid sands of external authority, was seen to rise again when those desert wastes had been passed. The witnesses to its presence are a goodly company, and their names are not limited to one land or church. Recalling the testimony of Francis of Assisi, of Thomas of Kempen, of Tauler, of the persecuted Spaniard Molinos, of the broad-minded but too submissive Fenelon, of the German peasant Jakob Bohme, of Madame Guyon, and many more, the Quaker has found in all a spirit confirming and supporting his own. And as the nineteenth century closes, he hears in the discourse of many earnest and spiritual evangelists the very thought of Fox. The two elements, the two sides, of the Truth which he proclaimed are here again,—reassertion of the Divine Inshining, and the demand for a pure and sincere life. Beset by opponents, afflicted by their own doubts and difficulties, perceiving that the spirit of dogma claims too much, and yet realizes far too little, the Christian leaders recur to original principles, and appeal once more to fundamental truth. The preaching of the early Friends is heard again all about us.

* * *

If we speak of the logical consequences of the Friends' fundamental principle, the question will be asked us, "What are they? What does the conception of the Divine Inshining necessarily imply." To answer this at length would unduly extend this paper, and to answer it with completeness would with even more certainty exceed the ability of the present writer. For, as has been said, the doctrine of the Inner Light, while it is simple, is far-reaching. He would be more than bold who would assign to the Spirit of God its metes and bounds. Yet there are certain results of the principle which seem at once natural and inevitable. Speaking on the point of doctrine briefly and guardedly, we may say that the Truth as Fox saw, and his followers see it, implies a benignant and merciful God, and forbids and dismisses the contrary thought. He who, as Peter perceived, is no respecter of persons; He who has left none of his children without a witness, but has imparted the principle of Truth to them all, must be a God of love, as John declared him, and as the world is coming to believe. Whatever, therefore, in the theologies of men, the catechisms and confessions, short or long, of churches or sects, proceeds in harmony with this conception of the Infinite Fatherhood, proceeds on the line of Quakerism; and, contrariwise, whatever scheme of doctrine is built upon the conception of an angry and aggrieved Diety, demanding to be appeased and propitiated, has no logical or natural relation to it. But, it is true, that as to this some Friends may differ. In doctrine it is hard to see eye to eye. Is there any church, where the mind is free, in which belief is uniform?

If it were needful to state more precisely, and more compactly, the faith of the Friends, I should say that it may be given under five headings. The first of these is fundamental to all religion. The second is the distinctive doctrine of Friends, without which there can be no Quakerism. And it, and the statements which follow it, as they vary from the declared creeds of other religious bodies, separate and differentiate Friends from the "churches" generally. I will call them:

THE FIRST FIVE PRINCIPLES OF QUAKERISM

FIRST—THE SUPREME BEING—Recognition and worship of God, the Creator and Ruler of All, attributing to Him the supreme qualities of Goodness, Love and Mercy.

SECOND—THE DIVINE IMMANENCE—Belief that God, thus good,, loving and merciful, directly reveals himself to the perceptions of man; that his light shines into our souls, if we admit it, and becomes thus "God's gift for man's salvation."

THIRD—THE SCRIPTURES—Confirming this immediate revelation of the Divine nature and purpose, the Scriptures record the visitations of God to the souls of men in past ages, and, in the New Testament, present to us the sublime and crowning truths of the Christian dispensation. We therefore revere the Scriptures, and desire to become possessors of the truth they contain, through the enlightenment of the same Spirit by which that truth was originally given forth by God. And without such enlightenment we believe none can obtain a true spiritual knowledge of them.

FOURTH—THE DIVINITY OF CHRIST—Convinced that the Divine nature, the Christ Spirit, the Word "which was in the beginning," dwelt in Jesus in an unparalleled, and, to our finite perceptions, an immeasurable degree we regard him (as John G. Whittier has formulated it) as "the highest possible manifestation of God in man."

FIFTH—THE CHRIST RULE IN DAILY LIFE—Desiring the guidance of the Divine Spirit which was in Jesus, embracing, from the force of his example, and through inward convincement, the infinite truth he illustrated and taught, Friends see in it the ideal of a religious life, and have striven to make real his teachings,— the Spirit, not the letter; Reality, not Form; Love, not Hatred; Brotherly Kindness, not Oppression; Moderation, not Excess; Simplicity, not Ostentation; Sincerity, not

Pretense; Truth, not Deceit; Economy, not Waste; and out of their sincere, if unperfected, endeavors to guide their daily acts by these Christian rules have logically and directly come their "testimonies," and most, if not all, of their "peculiarities."

These statements form a body of belief,—a positive and definite faith. They are not a Creed in the ordinary sense, first, because they do not proceed much beyond the simple and essential truths of the Christian religion; and, second, because they have never been officially presented as a "Confession" or "Declaration" of the Society. They will all be found distinctly set forth in the works of those who are recognized as the Society's founders and leaders, and all have been recognized by impartial and acute writers outside the Society as among the principles which give it character and reason for being.

* * *

Such a statement of faith, not proceeding to consider those theological formulae which necessarily are abstract and speculative, and which therefore are largely determined in each mind by many influences of temperament and surroundings, leaves all such to individual settlement. No one is to be persecuted for opinions concerning them. As experience has shown, at every step in recorded history, while there may be a substantial unity of Christian believers so far as concerns the essentials of Christianity, it is in vain that complete uniformity of belief is demanded. No measures of severity and cruelty, no shedding of blood or waste of treasure, has ever availed to bring about an agreement upon doctrinal opinions which are much removed from Primal Truth. Variations of view being thus natural and unavoidable—perhaps even desirable—the charity which is so great an element in Christian conduct must cover them all. This body of

Friends has happily been preserved by this rule for more than sixty years, finding brotherly love to prevail through "diligence to keep the unity of the Spirit in the bond of peace."

Such a unity of the Spirit is, indeed, a visible sign of the Quaker system. Such unity existed amongst the Christian societies of the Apostolic time. To revive the spirituality, the simplicity, of that day has been a Quaker aspiration. The doctrines and testimonies of the Friends, when faithfully maintained, says Samuel M. Janney, "constitute in their view a revival of primitive Christianity." The early and uncorrupted church had, he says, these characteristics: "A pure spiritual worship. A free gospel ministry. Religious liberty A testimony against war and oppression. A testimony against oaths. A testimony against vain fashions, corrupting amusements, and flattering titles." To the analysis thus made the system of Friends distinctly corresponds. The two are practically identical. The worship of the Friends, in silence, without form of ceremony, or pre-arrangement of services; their rejection or a professional ministry, or sacerdotal order; their charity and tolerance as to the non-essentials of doctrine; and their several testimonies against war and oppression, the taking of oaths, and vanities and corruptions of the world, are a near and close revival of the primitive church.

The Friends, it is true, have never accepted or observed the so-called "ordinances." Both ceremonials, the Baptism and the Supper, they decline. Both seem to them outward, and tending, like all ritual observances, to the worship of the symbol instead of the thing symbolized. So far as either of them has virtue or value it must be spiritual, not external or formal, and it is to the spiritual baptism and communion that the Friends aspire.

If it be demanded whether these ceremonies are not enjoined by Jesus, they think not, and they point to the fact that such injunction as he may appear to have given concerning them is far less definite and positive than his language in relation to the washing of one another's feet—a ceremonial which the churches with almost complete unanimity decline.

* * *

Finally, then, let us speak of those "logical consequences" of the Quaker principle which are expressed in Conduct. As to these there has been little variation of opinion among the different bodies of Friends. They have agreed that those who seek the divine guidance, and profess a submission to it, must give evidence of the fact in their daily walk. It is asked, says Samuel M. Janney, How we are to know the real Friend? "How shall we distinguish the members of Christ's spiritual body from those who merely pretend to his name?" There have been those who appeared in sheep's clothing, but in fact were ravening wolves. The test is easy. Jesus himself has supplied it. "By their fruits ye shall know them." "By this shall all men know ye are my disciples, if ye have love one to another."

Conduct, then, not profession, must be the evidence of Faith. A people spiritually minded must show spiritual fruits. "The fruit of the spirit," says Paul, "is love, joy, peace, long-suffering, kindness, meekness, temperance." "If we live in the spirit," he adds, "let us walk in the spirit."

Judged then, by their fruits, where do the Friends stand? It is not for them to assert their own merits. Yet they cannot shrink from the test,—that test, indeed, by which all profession of religion must ultimately be tried. The unfruitful tree that cumbereth the ground will be cut down. To that walk in life which Paul describes the Friends have endeavored to attain. Moved thereto by the teachings and the example of the Divine Master and by the promptings of the Divine influence within themselves, they found these to be evidences of the same Truth, supporting and confirming each other.

It has resulted, therefore, that the real Friend has been sober, earnest, upright and kindly. The world thus knows him. Happily there have been enough such in the Society to prove the practicability of such living, even under conditions far harder than those of today, and there have been enough, also, to exert an appreciable influence upon the opinion and action of the civilized world. The Friends have persevered. Their ethics, conforming to the list which Paul declared to the Galatians, have been those of Love, of Peace, of Long-suffering, of Kindness, of Meekness and of Temperance. Would this be anywhere denied? I think not. They have dwelt in Peace, and have testified to it. They have opposed War, and have testified against it. They have suffered for the Truth's sake, whenever persecution arose. They have shown brotherly kindness amongst themselves, and have rebuked the spirit of oppression wherever their voice could reach. They have upheld the beauty of a simple and sincere life, without vanity, without ostentation, without intemperance. Long ago they began to cleanse their own house of the evils which strong drink brought in. Long ago they declared and began practically to establish the equal rights of woman. It would require an extension of this analysis far beyond present possibilities to do justice to all these things. Each of the Testimonies of the Friends deserves its chapter, for each has its seed of life and virtue.

In the main, the Friends have been faithful to them all. Looking upon the world, with its shams and frauds, its methods of cruelty, deceit and oppression, its worship of Baal, its tribute to Ashtoreth, its bondage to Bacchus, we have the right to say that the Quaker testimonies have not only pointed the way to a better state, but have carried those who were faithful to them a good distance toward it.

* * *

If this be true, then, shall we not persevere? If this much has been achieved, is not more demanded? The Friends are few; shall they not increase? If the world's ills are so great, shall not the cure be everywhere applied? It is plain that the Principle of Truth which the Friends profess, and the system of ethics which has resulted from their profession, would bring in a new and better day. The establishment of Quakerism in its reality would leave no room for the antagonism of man and man, the conflicts of class and class, the wars of nation with nation. Were there no distempered ambition, were there no striving after excess, were all desires kept in just moderation, were there no greediness or grasping, no forgetfulness of the duties of self-restraint and self-sacrifice,—what would all this be but such as Quakerism demands, and yet what would it not do to bring peace on earth, and establish good-will amongst men?

To such a system, by whatever name it may be called, to whomsoever its origin may be referred, the world must ultimately come. Relief for the ills it suffers lies no other way. It can be saved only by the Divine processes. No mechanical readjustment of refractory and unregenerate elements will avail; there must be a sublime chemistry by which all will yield to the solvent of Love. In that day, who can doubt what power has supplied the solvent.

In the main, the Friends have been faithful to them all. Looking upon the world, with its shams and frauds, its methods of cruelty, deceit and oppression, its worship of Baal, its tribute to Ashtoreth, its bondage to Bacchus, we have the right to say that the Quaker testimonies have not only pointed the way to a better state, but have carried those who were faithful to them a good distance toward it.

* * *

If this be true, then, shall we not persevere? If this much has been achieved, is not more demanded? The Friends are few; shall they not increase? If the world's ills are so great, shall not the cure be everywhere applied? It is plain that the Principle of Truth which the Friends profess, and the system of ethics which has resulted from their profession, would bring in a new and better day. The establishment of Quakerism in its reality would leave no room for the antagonism of man and man, the conflicts of class and class, the wars of nation with nation. Were there no distempered ambition, were there no striving after excess, were all desires kept in just moderation, were there no greediness or grasping, no forgetfulness of the duties of self-restraint and self-sacrifice,—what would all this be but such as Quakerism demands, and yet what would it not do to bring peace on earth, and establish good-will amongst men?

To such a system, by whatever name it may be called, to whomsoever its origin may be referred, the world must ultimately come. Relief for the ills it suffers lies no other way. It can be saved only by the Divine processes. No mechanical readjustment of refractory and unregenerate elements will avail; there must be a sublime chemistry by which all will yield to the solvent of Love. In that day, who can doubt what power has supplied the solvent.

Lightning Source UK Ltd.
Milton Keynes UK
UKHW010622251122
412725UK00005B/513